Discover It Yourself

Nature at Risk

KINGFISHER
LONDON & NEW YORK

KINGFISHER
LONDON & NEW YORK

Published 2020 by Kingfisher
Published in the United States by
Kingfisher, 120 Broadway,
New York, NY 10271
Kingfisher is an imprint of
Macmillan Children's Books,
London
All rights reserved

Copyright © Macmillan Publishers
International Ltd 1999, 2020

Designed by Tall Tree
Illustrated by Diego Vaisberg/
Advocate Art

ISBN 978-0-7534-7645-1 (HB)
978-0-7534-7578-2 (PB)

First published in 1999 by
Kingfisher
This fully revised and updated
edition published
2020 by Kingfisher

Library of Congress Cataloging-in-
Publication data has been
applied for.

Kingfisher books are available for
special promotions and
premiums. For details contact:
Special Markets Department,
Macmillan, 120 Broadway, New
York, NY 1027

Printed in China
9 8 7 6 5 4 3 2 1
1TR/0420/WKT/UG/128MA

Contents

Where Animals Live 4
Keeping the Balance 6
Pollution Problems 8
Wonderful Woods 10
Forests in Danger 12
Rivers, Ponds, and Lakes 14
Save Our Seas 16
Farming Takes Over 18
City Living 20
Life on the Highways 22
Hunting and Collecting 24
Endangered Wildlife 26
Zoos Today 28
Pets and Performers 29
Make a Nature Reserve 30
Index 32

Make sure you have a grown-up to help whenever you see this sign.

Where Animals Live

Plants and animals are found almost everywhere on Earth—in the air, on the land, underground, and in the water. Each living thing belongs to a particular kind of place, called its habitat. For example, cacti grow in the desert, jellyfish are found in the ocean, parrots live in tropical forests. When people cut down trees to make way for roads and farms or pour harmful chemicals into the environment, they damage these habitats and destroy the wildlife.

Reefs at Risk

Coral reefs are home to many sea creatures and plants. Unfortunately, they are threatened by people who are polluting the oceans and damaging the coral reef's habitat.

Habitats

There are many different types of habitats in the world, from the tropical rain forests to the polar ice caps. This picture shows the kinds of animals that live in some of these habitats.

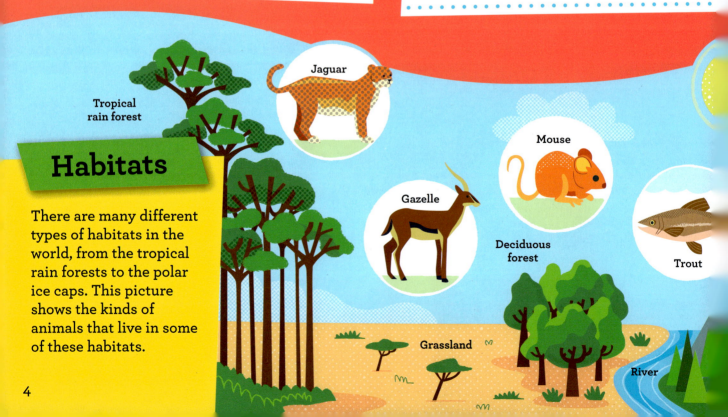

DISCOVER IT YOURSELF!

Find out what type of habitat woodlice like best.

1. With the help of an adult, find some pill bugs (woodlice) by looking under logs and bark.

2. Then spread a thin layer of cotton batting onto a small tray or box lid. Number the four quarters of the tray with labels, as shown here.

3. Cover half the tray with newspaper while you spray areas 1 and 2 with water. The cotton should be damp but not soaking wet.

4. Lay a piece of black paper cut to size over areas 1 and 3.

5. Now put your pill bugs in the middle of the tray and see which area they go to. Put the pill busgs back where you found them when you have finished.

? How It Works

You have divided the tray into four areas—(1) dark and damp, (2) light and damp, (3) dark and dry, and (4) light and dry. Pill bugs prefer dark, damp habitats, so they will go to area 1.

Eye Spy

If you want to see some animals in their natural habitat, turn over a log in your backyard or local park. How many different creatures can you find?

Eagle

Wolf

ountain

oniferous forest

Whale

Ocean

Polar bear

Ice cap

Keeping the Balance

Plants and animals that share the same habitat rely on each other for their survival. A delicate balance exists between them that depends largely on the amount of food available. Plants are able to make their own food, but animals have to find food in the environment. Some animals only eat plants—they are called herbivores. Other animals feed off the plant eaters. These are the carnivores, or meat eaters. But the balance is easily upset. For example, if fishermen catch too many sand eels, the seabirds that feed on the eels may die because they have no more food.

A Woodland Food Web

The diagram below shows "what eats what" in a wooded habitat. Energy for life begins with the Sun. Plants use the energy from sunlight to make food. Herbivores (in the orange band) eat the plants and are then eaten by the carnivores. Try to pick out a simple food chain—for example, an acorn is eaten by a mouse, which is then eaten by an owl. Can you figure out any other food chains?

DISCOVER IT YOURSELF!

See a food chain in action by trying out this experiment.

1. With the help of an adult, find a small leafy shoot that has a few aphids on it. (Try looking on roses or nasturtiums.) Put the shoot into a small bottle of water and plug the mouth of the bottle with tissue paper.

2. Put the bottle in a large glass jar. Cover the top with thin woven fabric—from an old T-shirt or a pair of pantyhose. Use a rubber band to hold it in place.

3. Watch the aphids for a few days through a magnifying glass. Can you see them sucking juices out of the plant?

4. Now put a ladybug into the jar and watch it feed off the aphids. Which animal is the herbivore, and which is the carnivore? Release the ladybug and greenfly when you have finished your experiment.

A Delicate Balance

Kestrels (a type of falcon) are predators of mice—that is, they feed on them. When there are a lot of mice, the kestrel has plenty of food and produces many young. But if the mouse population goes down, so does the number of kestrels.

Pollution Problems

One of the many threats to our wildlife is waste. In nature, waste materials such as dead plants and animals are quickly broken down and recycled. But much of the waste we produce is harmful and difficult to get rid of. Harmful waste is called pollution. Some of the most damaging pollution is caused by factories and cars. They produce fumes that turn the rain into acid. Acid rain has killed millions of trees. If we want to protect our environment, we must learn to cut down on the amount of pollution we are producing.

You can see waste almost everywhere you look—in the home, on the roads, in cities, and on farms. Garbage is buried in the countryside, liquid waste is poured into rivers and oceans, and harmful fumes are pumped into the air.

Acid rain

Factory fumes

Farming chemicals

Garbage

Transportation fumes

Waste from factories

Litter That Kills

Litter can be dangerous to wildlife. Sometimes small animals, such as mice and voles, climb into bottles, only to find they cannot get out again. Without food, they soon starve to death.

How Can We Help?

Don't drop litter. It may be a death trap.

Cut down on pollution by using the car less. Ride a bicycle or walk on short trips.

If you spot bad pollution, write a letter of complaint to your local government.

Algal Blooms

Sometimes you may find a thick green blanket of algae (tiny plants) floating on a river or pond. This is called an algal bloom. Eventually it leads to the death of fish living in the water. An algal bloom occurs when fertilizers from local farmland drain into a river or pond, causing the algae to grow very fast.

DISCOVER IT YOURSELF!

Find out how polluted your local stream or pond is by discovering which creatures live in the water.

1. With the help of an adult, sweep a dipping net through the water to catch some tiny animals.

2. Use this chart to identify your animals and find out how polluted the water is. Some animals can only live in unpolluted water, while others can survive in badly polluted water. Release any you find when you've finished.

WHAT TO LOOK FOR

Mayfly larva	Stone fly larva	No pollution
Caddis fly larva	Freshwater shrimp	Slight pollution
Water louse	Bloodworm	Medium pollution
Sludge worm	Rat-tailed maggot	Bad pollution
None found		Very bad

Wonderful Woods

Your local woods are important habitats because they are home to so many different plants and animals. The leaves and branches of the trees form a canopy high above the ground, providing shelter and food for birds and mammals. Leaf litter covers the woods floor. It is teeming with creepy-crawlies such as spiders, beetles, thrips, centipedes, and pill bugs. When woods are cut down to make way for roads, factories, farms, and expanding towns, all of these wonderful animals lose their homes.

DISCOVER IT YOURSELF!
Grow a tree from seed to plant in your garden.

1. Fill a small flowerpot or yogurt container with potting soil. Make a hole in the soil about 1.5 inches (4 centimeters) deep. Push a seed into the hole and cover it with soil.

2. Put your pot in a warm, sunny place and keep the soil damp. By spring, you may have a young sapling. Dig a small hole in the ground in a shady spot and plant your tree in it, along with its soil.

This picture shows just a few of the hundreds of different plants and animals that live in an oak tree. Small plants, such as mosses and ferns, grow on the trunk. Insects move among its branches. Small mammals come to the tree in search of food and shelter. And many birds build their nests in trees.

Bird

Squirrel

? How Can We Help?

- Plant your own tree (see opposite page).

- Join an organization that plants trees and cares for woods.

- If the woods near you is under threat, start a petition with family and friends asking your local government to save it.

DISCOVER IT YOURSELF!

Do a tree survey to find out as much as you can about a tree near you. Keep all your results in a special book.

1. Take a photograph of your tree in each season. Stand in the same spot each time to get the same view.

2. Collect a winter twig, a spring bud, a summer flower, and a fruit or seed in the fall.

3. Find out how old your tree is by measuring around the trunk about 3 feet (1 meter) above the ground. Count one year for every inch (2.5 centimeters) you measure.

4. Take leaf and bark rubbings using a crayon and paper. Press some leaves in your book as well—one for each season.

5. Use a field guide to identify what kinds of plants and animals are living in and around your tree.

Forests in Danger

Trees are very useful plants. As well as being home to a wealth of wildlife, their wood can be used for making paper, for building homes and furniture, and as fuel. Also, when plants make food from sunlight, they use up a gas called carbon dioxide and release the gas oxygen. People breathe in oxygen and breathe out carbon dioxide, and trees help balance the level of these gases in the air. Yet all around the world, forests are rapidly being destroyed for timber or to grow crops.

Eye Spy

Go into each room at home and see how many things you can find that come from trees. Here are some ideas.

DISCOVER IT YOURSELF!

Try this simple experiment to see how plants give off a gas.

1. Fill a bowl or glass tank with water. Put a glass or jar into the water and tilt it so that all the air escapes.

2. Place some pondweed in the glass without letting any air back in. (You can buy pondweed at a pet store.)

3. Turn the glass upside down in the water and set it on three small blobs of modeling clay. Make sure you leave a small gap underneath the glass.

4. Leave the tank for a few days in a warm, sunny place. Watch the gas bubbling off the plant and collecting at the top of the glass. This gas is oxygen, produced by the plant as it makes food.

Rain forests are home to at least three-quarters of all the world's wildlife. Millions of different kinds of plants and animals live there, but many of them have not yet been discovered.

Rain Forest Medicines

Did you know that many of our medicines are made from plants that grow in the rain forest? Drugs made from this rosy periwinkle are used to treat leukemia. Unless we save the remaining rain forests, we will lose many useful plants that could save lives.

Rosy periwinkle

? How Can We Help?

- Don't waste paper—you are also wasting trees.

- Collect newspapers and cardboard for recycling.

- When people buy new furniture, they should check that it is not made of wood from the rain forests, such as teak or mahogany.

Rivers, Ponds, and Lakes

Clean fresh water is home to a wide variety of wildlife. Animals such as fish, snails, crayfish, and insects live in the water itself; dragonflies and mayflies skim across the surface; water birds live close by; and water plants flourish on the banks. But many of our rivers, ponds, and lakes have become polluted by waste chemicals that pour into them from farms and factories. Sometimes only the hardiest plants and animals survive in the filthy water.

A healthy river is teeming with wildlife living in and around the water. A polluted stretch of river has little life in it. The dirty water often smells and may be full of all kinds of litter. An algal bloom may float on the water's surface.

Fisherman's Threat

Waterbirds sometimes get tangled in fishing lines left on riverbanks by careless fishermen. The birds may die if the line gets too tight around their throats.

Cleanup Campaign

Many young people spend some of their spare time helping to clean up a local river or pond, making it much safer for wildlife. Find out if there is a cleanup campaign near you that you can join.

DISCOVER IT YOURSELF!

Make your own pond dipping net so you can investigate the wildlife in your nearest pond or river. And make sure you go with an adult.

1. Ask an adult to cut a piece off a metal coat hanger about 2.5 feet (7.5 centimeters) long. Bend the wire into a circle, leaving 2 inches (5 centimeters) at each end, then poke the ends into a bamboo stick. Tape it in place with insulating tape.

2. Cut the legs off some pantyhose. Sew the cut edges together to make a "bag" out of the waist.

3. Fold the top edge of the pantyhose over the wire and sew it down to hold the bag firmly in place to complete your net.

4. Take a large plastic container with you to keep your animals in, plus a magnifying glass. When you have caught some animals in your net, do not pick them up with your fingers—you may squash them. Instead, turn the net inside out and lower it into the water inside the container. Always put the animals back when you have finished looking at them.

Save Our Seas

Today our oceans are under threat. We rely on the seas to provide us with food, particularly fish. But we are catching far too many fish, so their numbers are going down rapidly. Pollution is a problem, too. For many years, people thought that getting rid of waste at sea was safe and that it would be quickly diluted. But poisons build up in the water and affect the health of sea animals. All over the world, dolphins and seals are dying from new diseases, and fish are found with strange-looking growths on their skin.

Blue Planet

Pacific Ocean

Almost three-quarters of Earth's surface is covered by water. Yet we manage to pollute much of it and take fish stocks dangerously low.

Animals such as dolphins, turtles, and sharks often get caught up in fishing nets. Purse seine nets are like huge bags, whereas drift nets are more like curtains. Both of these nets can be death traps. Long lines are much better because they only catch the fish that are wanted.

Purse seine net

Drift net

DISCOVER IT YOURSELF!

Do this simple test to see how oil damages a bird's feathers.

1. Collect two feathers. Then rub a few drops of bicycle oil or lubricating oil onto one of the feathers using a cotton ball.

2. Pour a few drops of water on each feather and see what happens.

Clean feather

Oily feather

 How It Works

The drops of water on the clean feather roll off because the feather is waterproof. The oil destroys the waterproofing, so the water soaks into the oily feather and spoils its shape. Seabirds with oily feathers cannot fly or dive and soon die from cold and hunger.

More Things to Try

The barbs of a feather are attached to one another with hooks, rather like Velcro. Oil damages the feathers so that the hooks no longer work, and the bird cannot fly. You can see the hooks on a feather by using a magnifying glass. Try breaking the hooks apart and then joining them up again like a zip. This zip effect is useful, because even if the feathers break apart in stormy weather, the bird can always "zip" them up again by preening them into shape.

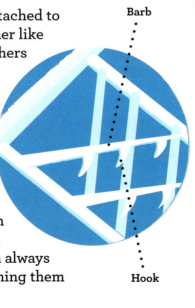

Barb

Hook

Oil Tankers

Oil tankers move millions of tons of oil around the world each year. When there is an accident, oil spills into the sea, where it causes terrible damage to wildlife. Thousands of seabirds may die. If the birds are rescued quickly, the oil can be removed from their feathers by washing them carefully in detergents such as dishwashing detergent.

Farming Takes Over

The number of people in the world has increased rapidly over the past two hundred years, and it is still increasing. All these extra mouths need food to eat, and farming has had to keep up with the demand. Natural habitats are destroyed to make way for huge fields. Chemicals are sprayed onto the fields to increase the yield (output). There are fertilizers to feed the crops, and pesticides to kill pests. But these chemicals cause pollution, and pesticides kill more than just the pests.

Free-Range

Many farm animals live indoors, packed together with no room to move. But on some farms, animals roam free outdoors. These animals are called free-range.

Natural Pockets

To avoid using harmful pesticides, some farmers grow small pockets of woods in the corners of their fields. Many of the animals that live there feed on the pests.

On a farm, the huge fields are usually planted with a single crop and sprayed with chemicals. Few plants and animals are found living here. Combines are used to cut down crops. But they also destroy small animals that get in their way. In comparison to farmland, natural meadows and woods are rich in wildlife. It is important to protect these habitats.

? How Can We Help?

- Eat organic foods—they are grown without chemicals that harm wildlife.

- Eat free-range eggs and meat—the animals they come from are kept in comfortable conditions.

DISCOVER IT YOURSELF!

Worms are farmers' friends. As they burrow through the soil, they mix it all up and let air into it. This helps keep the soil healthy. You can watch worms at work by making a "wormery."

1. Take a large glass jar and fill it with three layers of different bedding, such as gravel or sand, mud, or ordinary soil.

2. Add a layer of leaves. Then put four or five worms on top.

3. Wrap black paper around your wormery to keep it dark, and make sure the soil is kept moist. Check it after a day or two to see what has happened. Release the worms when you have finished.

19

City Living

Modern cities are jungles of concrete and asphalt. Yet a city habitat is very different from a natural habitat such as a forest. Despite this, wildlife can be found even in the middle of the world's busiest cities. Animals are attracted to cities because there is a vast and never-ending supply of free food, such as the food that gets thrown out with our garbage. Many birds and mammals make their homes in parks and tree-lined roads, whereas animals such as rats and mice live beneath the cities in the sewers and drains.

Eye Spy

You have to look pretty carefully to spot some city dwellers. Old walls may be home to a host of tiny plants and animals. How many creatures can you find living on a wall?

Raccoon

Fox

Rat

Polar bears are among the largest visitors to towns—and the most dangerous! Many are attracted by the free supply of food that can be found in garbage dumps.

Storks often nest on rooftops in northern European towns.

DISCOVER IT YOURSELF!

Attract birds to your town garden or school grounds by putting out bird food. Use this recipe to make your own bird food.

To make a coconut cake, ask an adult to melt 9 ounces (250 grams) of lard or suet. Mix in 18 ounces (500 grams) of mixed raisins, peanuts, bread and cake crumbs, sunflower seeds, and oatmeal. Put the mix into half a coconut shell and let it set before you hang it up outside.

Make a string of whole peanuts by threading the nuts together using a large needle and strong thread.

Deer

Stork

Pigeon

Life on the Highways

Roads reach almost everywhere. Roadsides are often planted with grass and trees to make them look attractive. Although there is pollution from car fumes, these areas are usually free from harmful pesticides. So roadsides have formed new habitats for many plants and animals. The plants attract insects, birds, and mammals. Some birds feed on dead insects that bounce off car windshield. Other birds and foxes feed on animals that are killed on the road.

Beware!

Special road signs are used to warn drivers about animals crossing the road. This protects the animals but also prevents drivers from having accidents.

Save a Toad

Every spring, toads travel to their breeding ponds. They often have to cross roads, and many get killed. Now people help toads by carrying them safely across the roads.

Roadsides attract many plants and animals that do not mind living so close to traffic.

DISCOVER IT YOURSELF!

Make a highway habitat mobile that includes a hawk and four mice.

1. Trace the shapes on this page and transfer them on to stiff cardboard. You will need one hawk, four mice, and two of each of the fruits. Cut your shapes out.

2. Paint or color the shapes on both sides. Use a felt-tip pen or marker to add the details.

3. Ask an adult to help you pierce holes in your shapes as marked on the pattern. Then string your mobile together using a needle and thick thread. Follow the diagram below to see where each of the pieces should go.

4. Hang your mobile up and watch the hawk hovering as it looks for mice!

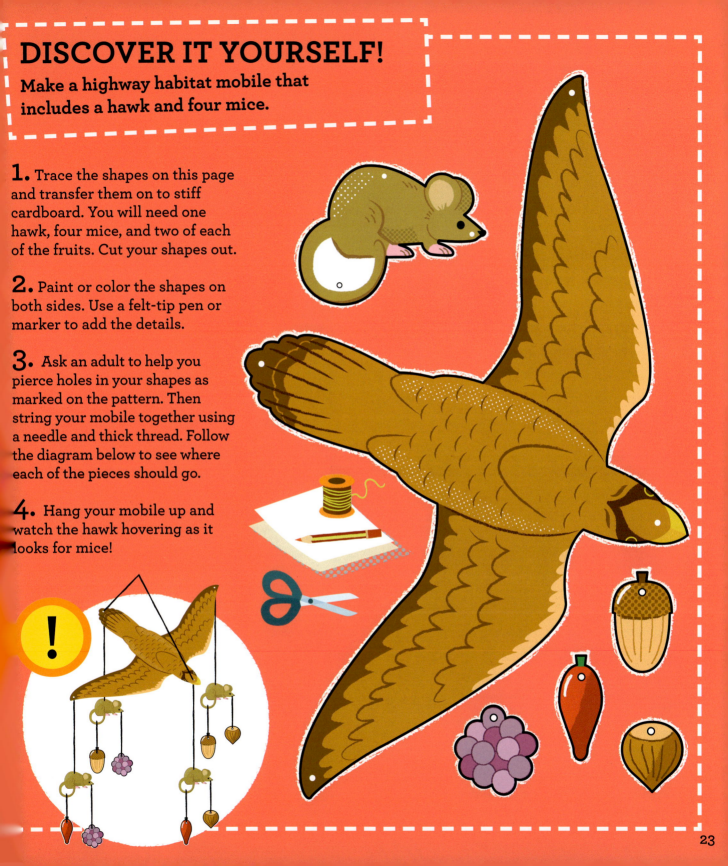

Hunting and Collecting

People have hunted animals for food and skins for thousands of years. Today animals are also hunted for sport or for their horns, tusks, bones, or fur. Hunting and collecting threatens the survival of many creatures. There are now laws to protect some animals, such as the law banning the trade in elephant ivory. Sadly, animals such as big cats are still hunted, even though they are protected by law. The poachers can make a lot of money by selling their fur.

Eye Spy

When you are on vacation, watch out for souvenirs and other objects that are made from wild animals, such as ivory objects, crocodile-skin bags, corals, sponges, and shells. Would you want to buy any of these?

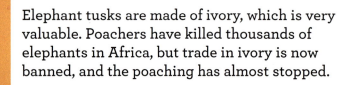

Elephant tusks are made of ivory, which is very valuable. Poachers have killed thousands of elephants in Africa, but trade in ivory is now banned, and the poaching has almost stopped.

DISCOVER IT YOURSELF!

Unlike hunting, tracking animals does not hurt them, and it can be great fun.

1. Next time you go for a walk, look for any tracks or signs left by animals. See if you can figure out what kind of animal each belongs to. Things to look for include tufts of fur, feathers, footprints, leftover food, animal footpaths in the grass, and droppings.

2. Small mammals have their own particular way of eating nuts and cones, so look out for these signs.

3. You can usually recognize animal droppings by their shape. Also look for fur caught on barbed wire.

4. Each animal has its own set of footprints. They often show up best in mud or snow. See if you can find any of these footprints.

How Can We Help?

- Don't collect birds' eggs, butterflies, wild flowers, or any other living thing.
- If you collect wild animals such as snails or pond creatures to study, keep them only for a short time and always return them to their natural habitat afterward.
- Don't kill animals just because you don't like them—spiders, moths, ants, and slugs are just as important as bigger animals.
- Don't wear fur. Too many big cats such as leopards and tigers have been killed for their beautiful fur. The fur only looks good when worn by the cat—not when worn by a person.

Fur caught on barbed wire
Deer droppings

Hazelnut eaten by a squirrel
Hazelnut eaten by a mouse

cone eaten by a squirrel

Fox dropping

Rabbit droppings

Fox print

Deer prints

Squirrel prints (back paws)

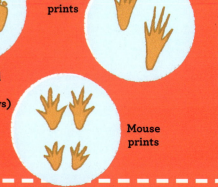
Rat prints
Mouse prints

Endangered Wildlife

Many plants and animals have disappeared completely from Earth. That is, they have become extinct. Sometimes this happens naturally. Dinosaurs may have died out because of a sudden change in climate. But many species are now extinct because of humans. Destruction of habitat is the biggest threat to wildlife. It has made animals such as the giant panda become endangered. This means that there are only a few thousand individuals, or even fewer, left in the world.

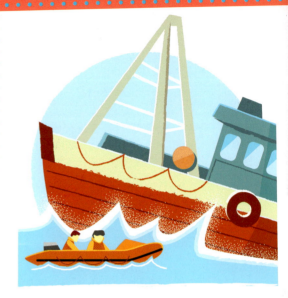

Special organizations such as Greenpeace try to protect endangered animals. Here, they are trying to stop whaling.

Extinct!

The dodo was a large, flightless bird that lived on Mauritius. An easy catch for sailors, the last one was killed in 1700.

Running Wild

Wolves were once a common sight in Europe and the United States. But they caught sheep and cattle, so they were shot by farmers. They are now being reintroduced in some of the places where they once roamed wild.

Many well-known animals are endangered. If these animals are not protected and their habitats conserved, they may soon disappear forever. Imagine what the world would be like without tigers, rhinoceroses, elephants, pandas, and whales!

In the Country

Many of us can do little to help tigers and whales, but we can all help conserve wildlife closer to home by following a few simple rules when we go out to the country.

- Do not pick any wildflowers, even if there are plenty of them.
- Stay on the paths or trails so you do not trample wild flowers.
- Keep your dog on a leash if there are nesting birds or other animals around.
- Close gates so that farm animals do not escape.

Zoos Today

For a long time, zoos were simply places where animals were kept in small cages to entertain the public. The modern zoo, however, has a far more important role. Many zoos keep endangered animals. This is often the only way to stop an animal from becoming extinct. The zoos breed them in special enclosures. Eventually, they may be able to release some of the animals back into the wild.

Sometimes a mother animal abandons her baby, so zookeepers have to rear it by hand. This baby koala is only a few days old.

Modern zoos have large enclosures where the animals can live together. The brown bear above is catching salmon from a stream in its enclosure. Older zoos have small brick cages. Animals have little room to move around and are often kept by themselves for their whole lives.

Pets and Performers

Nowadays people keep many exotic pets, such as snakes, monkeys, and spiders. In the past, it was also common to keep performing animals to entertain audiences. Dolphins, elephants, lions, and many others were trained to do tricks. But this became unpopular with the public because the animals were often cruelly treated.

DISCOVER IT YOURSELF!

Make your own snail house and keep some pet snails for a few days.

1. Find a cake tin lid. Cut a strip of acetate 12 inches (30 centimeters) wide and long enough to line the lid. Put the acetate in the lid as shown and tape it in place. Make an acetate lid to fit and pierce holes in it.

2. Put soil, stones, leaves, and twigs into the snail tank, then add your snails. Tape the acetate lid on top. Be sure to keep your tank damp and give your snails plenty of leaves to eat.

Exotic Pets

ny pets come from faraway
es. They are often caught in the
d and transported to pet stores
he other side of the world.
ge number of them may die
ng the long journey.

Make a Nature Reserve

It is easy to attract wildlife into our backyards, especially birds. Climbing plants and hedges give the birds shelter, an upturned garbage lid makes a good birdbath, and plants such as sunflowers and purple cornflowers provide food. Let the grass grow long if you want to attract creepy-crawlies—they prefer long grass. Even flowerpots or a pile of logs can be home to a surprising number of animals.

Attracting Butterflies

- Buddleia, poppies, sedum, zinnas, and lavender are all good for attracting butterflies, which feed on their sweet nectar.
- Asters, violets, and cabbages are good food plants for caterpillars.

Turn a corner of your backyard into a nature reserve. With the help of an adult, build a pond to attract a wealth of wildlife, from snails and dragonflies to frogs, newts, and maybe the occasional duck. Piles of logs will house insects, centipedes, spiders, and toads. And a compost heap for kitchen waste and grass cuttings will become home to worms, snakes, and toads.

DISCOVER IT YOURSELF!

Build a garden pond to attract water creatures.

1. Ask an adult to dig a hole in the ground about 1.5 feet (0.5 meters) deep and 5 feet (1.5 meters) across. Gently slope the sides of the hole down to the bottom.

2. Line the hole with sand about 2.5 inches (6 centimeters) deep or with layers of newspaper. Lay a sheet of thick plastic, about 6.5 feet (2 meters) square, on top.

3. Anchor the sheet with slabs of rock around the edges, as shown.

4. Buy a pond plant from a garden center or nursery, such as a water lily, and put it in the centre of your pond. You will also need some pondweed to provide the water with oxygen. Now fill the pond with water.

5. Dip in your pond every week to see what new animals are living there. Remember to keep the filled up with water in dry weather.

More Things to Try

If you do not have a backyard, you may still be able to put out a window box filled with flowers to attract wildlife. Plants such as phlox, black-eyed Susan, thyme, petunia, and candytuft provide plenty of color and scent and will attract lots of insects, especially butterflies.

Index

acid rain 8
algal blooms 9, 14

backyard nature reserve 30–31
bird food 21
butterflies 30, 31

carbon dioxide 12
carnivores 6
chemicals 4, 14, 18, 19
cities 20–21
cleanup campaigns 15
collecting animals and plants 24, 25
coral reefs 4
creepy-crawlies 5, 7, 9, 10, 14, 15, 30

dinosaurs 26
dodo 26

elephant ivory 24
endangered animals 26–27, 28
extinction 26, 28

farming 9, 18–19

fishing 6, 14, 16
flowers 25, 27, 30, 31
food chains 6–7
free-range farm animals 18, 19
fur 25

habitat destruction 4, 18, 26
habitats 4–5, 6, 10, 20, 22
herbivores 6
highway habitat mobile 23
hunting 24

kestrels 7
killing animals 24, 25

medicines 13
mice 6, 7, 8

oil spills 17
organic food 19
oxygen 12

performing animals 29
pest control 18
pets, exotic 29
pill bugs 5, 10

poachers 24
polar bears 21
pollution 4, 8–9, 14, 16, 17, 18, 22
pond dipping 15, 31

rain forests 4, 13
rivers, ponds, and lakes 9, 14–15, 30, 31
roadsides 22–23

seabirds 6, 17
seas 4, 16–17
seeds, planting 10
snail house 29
storks 21

toads 22
tracks, animal 25
trees 4, 10–11, 12, 13

waste 8–9, 20, 21
window boxes 31
wolves 27
woodls 6, 10–11, 18, 19
wormery 19

zoos 28